PULL AHEAD BOOKS
Forces of Nature

Blizzards

by Lisa Bullard

Lerner

Lerner Books • London • New York • Minneapolis

For my brother Dan, with love, for sharing all of those snow days with me

Photo Acknowledgements
The images in this book are used with the permission of: © Photodisc/Getty Images, p 1, all backgrounds; © Robert Giroux/Getty Images, p 4; © Christopher Pillitz/Reportage/Getty Images, p 6; © David Jay Zimmerman/CORBIS, p 7; © John Beatty/Photo Researchers, Inc., p. 8; AP Photo/Peter M Fredin, p 9; © Reuters/CORBIS, pp 10, 12; AP Photo/Charlie Neibergall, p 11; © Colin McPherson/CORBIS, p 14; AP Photo/Wyoming Highway Patrol, p 15; © Ralph Orlowski/Getty Images, p 16; © China Photos/Getty Images, p 18; © SIU/Visuals Unlimited, p 19; © Scientifica/Visuals Unlimited, p 20; © KEN HAWKINS/CORBIS SYGMA, p 22; AP Photo/The Patriot-News, Amiran White, p 24; © Stockbyte/Getty Images, p 26; © Jochen Sand/Riser/Getty Images, p 27; © Bill Hauser/Independent Picture Service, p 28.
Front Cover: AP Photo/Benny Snyder.

First published in the United Kingdom in 2010 by
Lerner Books,
Dalton House,
60 Windsor Avenue,
London SW19 2RR

Website address: www.lernerbooks.co.uk

This edition was updated and edited for UK publication by Discovery Books Ltd., First Floor, 2 College Street, Ludlow, Shropshire SY8 1AN

Words in **bold type** are explained in a glossary on page 3

British Library Cataloguing in Publication Data

Bullard, Lisa
Blizzards. - 2nd ed. - (Pull ahead books. Forces of nature)
1. Blizzards - Juvenile literature
I. Title
551.5'55

ISBN-13: 978 0 7613 4388 2

Printed in China

Table of Contents

What Is a Blizzard?

Cold winds blast. Cars are buried under snowdrifts. Why has the world turned white?

This monster storm is called a **blizzard**.

Snowstorms are very cold and have heavy snow. But not all snowstorms are blizzards.

It takes a strong wind to turn a
snowstorm into a blizzard.

A scientist uses a special tool to measure wind speed.

Blizzard winds blow at 56 kilometres per hour (35 miles per hour) or more. They last for at least three hours.

The strong winds swirl any falling snow.
The winds also pick up more snow
from the ground.

Snow swirling in the air makes it very hard to see. People can become lost while walking or driving.

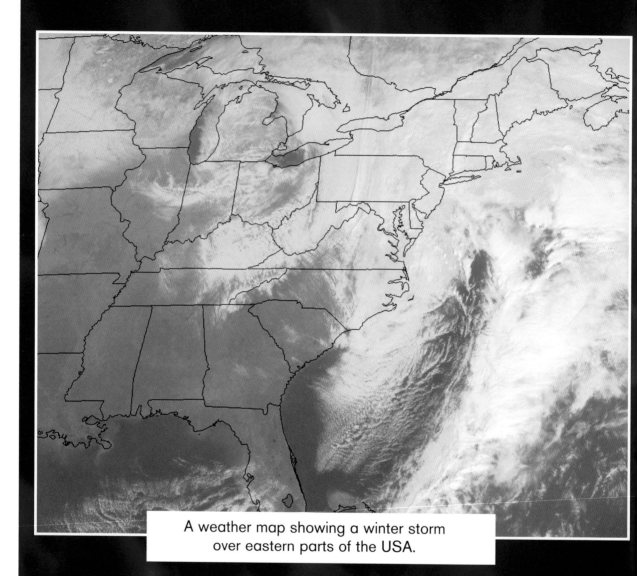

A weather map showing a winter storm over eastern parts of the USA.

Where Blizzards Happen

Blizzards happen most often in the countries of Canada, Russia and the United States. In the United Kingdom snowstorms and blizzards mostly happen in the north of the country.

Most snowstorms do not become blizzards. There might be only one blizzard in the UK every few years.

A man battles through a blizzard in Scotland.

But these storms can kill people.

Heavy snow made this roof cave in.

Dangers of Blizzards

Snow and ice make roads very slippery and some people die in car accidents. The roofs of buildings can cave in from the heavy snow and crush people. Hikers may become lost far from home. During a blizzard, the **temperature** can become very cold.

Strong winds make the air feel even colder. This is known as **wind chill**. People and animals should not stay outside too long in this weather. They could freeze to death.

If you have to go outside during a blizzard, you should cover up as much of your skin as possible.

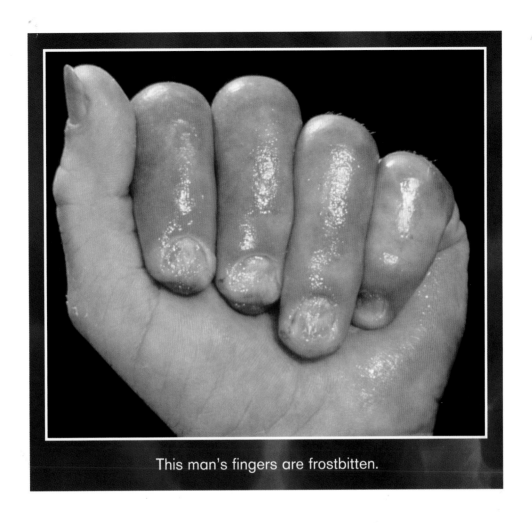

This man's fingers are frostbitten.

People can get **frostbite**. The cold freezes a part of their bodies. Frostbite often happens to fingers, toes or ears.

Meteorologists use computers to track storms.

Tracking Blizzards

Scientists who study the weather are called meteorologists. They try to warn people before a blizzard strikes. They use computers and other tools to track storms. But they cannot always tell when or where a blizzard will hit. Blizzards often take people by surprise.

This girl in Atlanta, Georgia, slides in the snow left behind by the Storm of the Century.

Storm of the Century

In the USA in 1993 a huge blizzard surprised many people. It was called the Storm of the Century. The blizzard hit 26 states. Heavy snow fell in states that rarely get snow. Winds blew over 160 kph (100 mph) at times. More than 1.2 metres of snow fell in some places. The storm even caused several **tornadoes**. More than 270 people died.

A **snowmobile** is used to drive through a street
that is covered with snow.

Staying Safe

People who live in cold places watch for blizzard warnings. They stay at home. They wear many layers of clothing to keep warm. They try not to drive on slippery roads. Some people have snowmobiles. They use them to get around when roads are covered with snow.

Snow is an important source of the
Earth's water. But the wildest
snowstorms are also dangerous.

Don't take chances in a blizzard. Wait inside until it is safe to go out and play!

Blizzard Weather

Blizzards can form when a warm, moist weather system meets a cold, dry weather system.

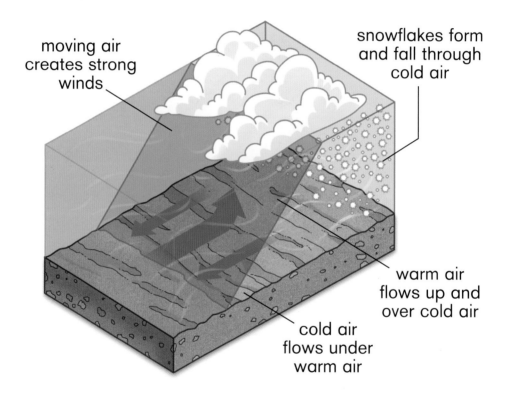

moving air creates strong winds

snowflakes form and fall through cold air

warm air flows up and over cold air

cold air flows under warm air

Blizzard Facts

- There are different stories about where the word *blizzard* comes from. Long ago, it was used to describe things like a hard punch or a gunshot. Then, in the 1870s, an American newspaper used *blizzard* to describe a terrible snowstorm. Soon that became the major meaning of the word.

- In January 1881 a blizzard hit the UK. It was the worst blizzard there has ever been in southern parts of the country. About 60 centimetres of snow fell in Dorset, and the Isle of Wight recorded nearly a metre of snow on the ground. There were huge piles of snow in London, too.

- Wind chill measures how cold it is when the wind blows. Let's say the temperature falls to −15°C and blizzard winds are 56 kph (35 mph). The wind chill then equals −29°C. Uncovered skin can freeze in just 1 minute.

- Wearing a hat is very important when it is cold. People lose lots of heat through their heads.

Further Reading

Books

Barraclough, Sue. *Weather and Seasons* (Investigate) Heinemann Library, 2008.

Chambers, Catherine. *Blizzard*. (Wild Weathers) Heinemann Library, 2007.

Ganeri, Anita. *Stormy Weather* (Horrible Geography) Scholastic, 2008.

Websites

BBC, What is weather?
http://www.bbc.co.uk/schools/whatisweather/
Learn about different types of weather around the world, and see how much you know by taking the weather quiz.

Weather Wiz Kids
http://www.weatherwizkids.com/winter_storms.htm
Find out how snowstorms and blizzards form and learn more about a wide range of other forces of nature.

Glossary

blizzard: a snowstorm with strong winds. Blizzard winds blow at about 56 kph (35 mph) or more for at least three hours. The winds blow snow that makes it hard to see more than 400 m in front of you.

frostbite: an injury caused when part of the body freezes. Frostbite often affects a person's fingers or toes first.

meteorologists: scientists who study the weather

snowmobile: a machine that people can drive over snow

temperature: a measure of how hot or cold it is. Temperature can be measured in degrees Fahrenheit (°F) or Celsius (°C).

tornadoes: dangerous, spinning windstorms

wind chill: a measure of how cold the wind makes the air temperature feel

Index

First published in the United States of America in 2009
Text copyright © 2009 by Lerner Publishing Group, Inc.